THE ASSYRIAN EMPIRE'S THREE ATTEMPTS TO RULE THE WORLD

Ancient History of the World

Children's Ancient History

BABY PROFESSOR
EDUCATION KIDS

Speedy Publishing LLC

40 E. Main St. #1156

Newark, DE 19711

www.speedypublishing.com

Copyright 2017

The Assyrian Empire was the greatest, and one of the longest-lasting political bodies in Mesopotamia, the area in the Middle East centered on the Tigris and Euphrates rivers. Three times the Assyrians were on the edge of ruling the whole known world! Let's find out about that.

THE ASSYRIANS BEGIN

Assyria started around a little community called Ashur, north-east of Babylon. The city had had people living in it from around 3000 BCE, but its formal history starts around 1900, when the first great temple was built. This probably marks a change in lifestyle for the Assyrians, moving from "people who live in tents", following their flocks, to people who mainly live in houses in a community.

BABYLON, IRAQ

ANCIENT BABYLONIA AND ASSYRIA SCULPTURE

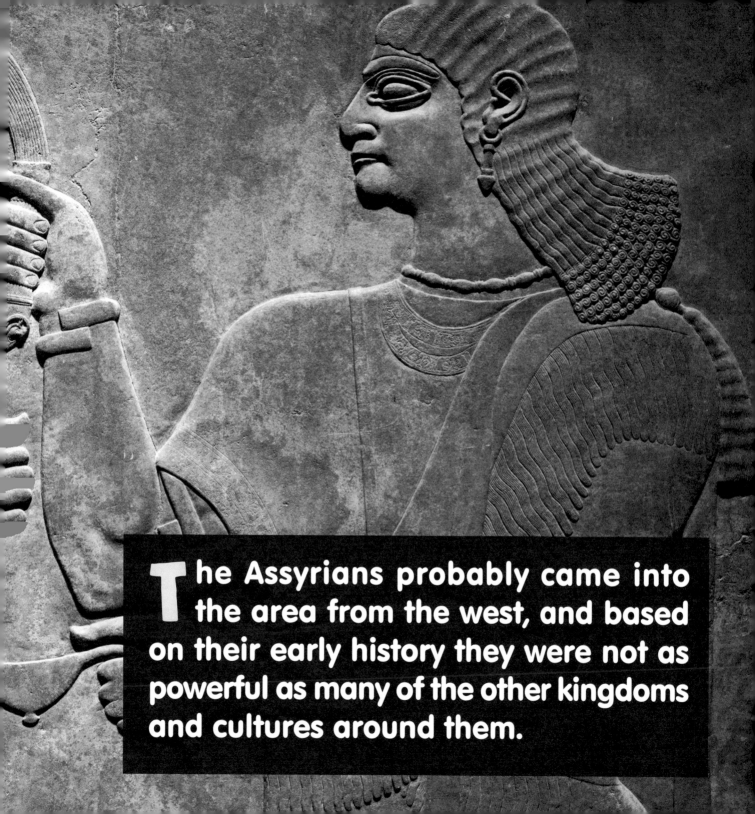

The Assyrians probably came into the area from the west, and based on their early history they were not as powerful as many of the other kingdoms and cultures around them.

THE OLD KINGDOM

Ashur grew rich on trade and started to expand. Trading with kingdoms in what is now Turkey gave the Assyrians access to iron and other raw materials. The iron weapons of the Assyrian army gave them an early advantage over the armies of the other kingdoms in the region.

THE CONQUEST OF THE AMORITES

The dominant group in the area, the Amorites, were driven out by a new group, the Hatti, in the eighteenth century. The Hatti were conquered, and merged with, the Hitties by around 1700 BCE. But by now the Assyrians were starting to worry about the growing Babylonian Empire, to their southwest.

The Babylonians, under King Hammurabi, conquered the whole area, including Assyria, by 1750 BCE. When the Babylonian Empire fell apart soon after, Assyria attempted to expand to fill the power gap. However, its kings were not up to the task. The best the kingdom could manage was stable borders, a bit larger than it had started with, by about 1700.

HAMMURABI

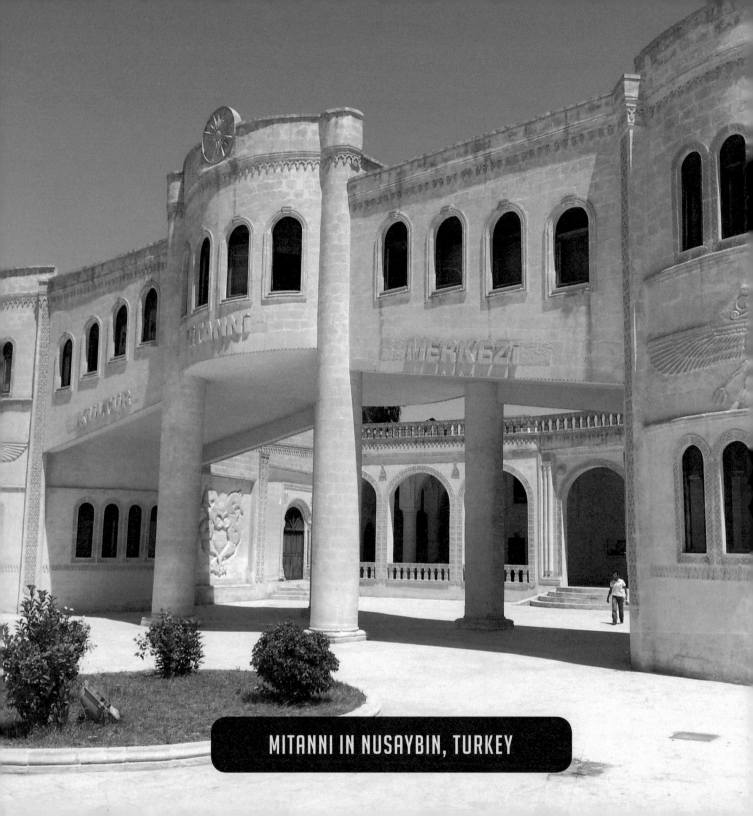

MITANNI IN NUSAYBIN, TURKEY

THE MIDDLE KINGDOM

The kingdom of the Mitanni grew in what is now eastern Turkey and took control of northern Mesopotamia, including Assyria. Then the Hittites defeated the Mitanni in the fourteenth century. Under this change, Assyria started to expand again. Assyria fought a series of wars against both Hittites and Mitanni, slowly gaining territory, until around 1350, when Assyria won a great military victory.

The next expansion was to the north and south, around 1280. Assyria captured the Hittite homelands and strongholds. At this point, Assyria had managed to bring a larger area under peaceful rule by a single government than any other kingdom in the Middle East had managed. The kingdom was wealthy and able to support a strong government and a capable army.

THE LION GATE OF THE HATTUSA THAT IS THE CAPITAL OF THE HITTITE CIVILIZATION, CORUM

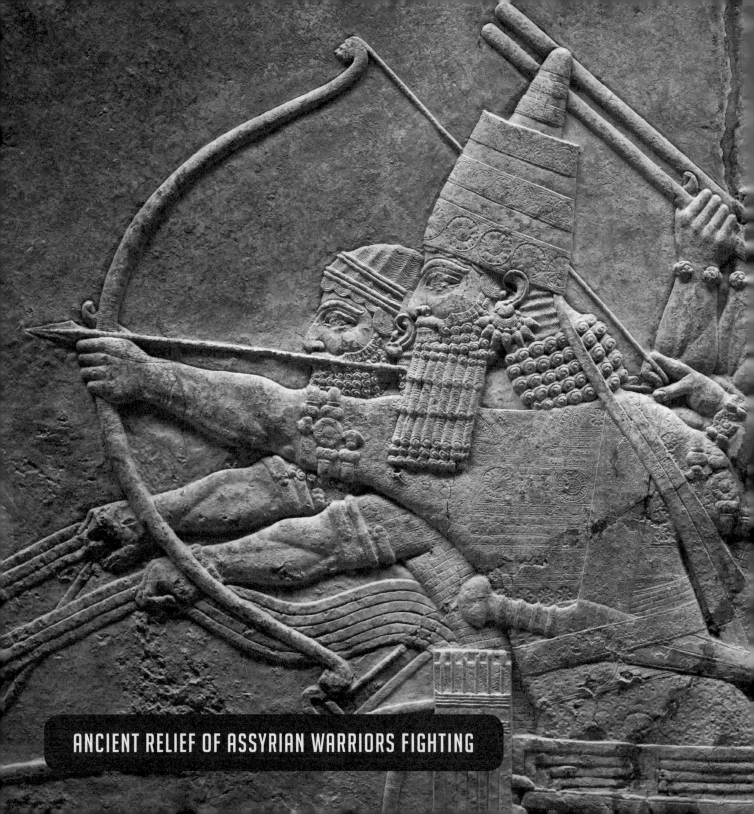

ANCIENT RELIEF OF ASSYRIAN WARRIORS FIGHTING

One of the central policies of the Assyrians, when they conquered a region, was to relocate a large part of the conquered people to a different part of the empire. This was both to reduce the threat of revolts and independence movements, and to move workers to areas that needed both trained and untrained labor. In the Baby Professor book The Heart-Shattering Facts about the Trail of Tears you can learn how the United States forcibly relocated Native Americans in order to develop their lands. The Assyrian policy seems to have been much gentler, and did not involve so much misery for the people who had to move to a new part of the empire.

By 1210 BCE the Assyrians had completely absorbed the Mitanni. They then went on to conquer the Hittites and Elamites. While being effective and even cruel in battle, the Assyrians also worked hard to preserve the knowledge, scientific learning, and history of the people they conquered.

CHOGHA ZANBIL IS AN ANCIENT ELAMITE COMPLEX IN THE KHUZESTAN PROVINCE OF IRAN

TIGLATH PILESAR I IN HIS CHARIOT

Around 1200 BCE most of the kingdoms of the Middle East suffered an economic and political collapse. Assyria did not expand during this time, but it does not seem to have suffered as its neighbor kingdoms did. This period of much activity but little growth lasted until 1115, when Tiglath Pilesar I became king.

Tiglath Pilesar I was energetic in warfare, in construction projects, and in creating great libraries that gathered together the knowledge of the civilized world. He won battles as far west as the shore of the Mediterranean Sea. He built both palaces and libraries in the capital. He issued a set of laws, partly modeled on the Code of Hammurabi of Babylon. He was among the first kings to create parks and gardens, and collections of exotic plants brought from far-off lands.

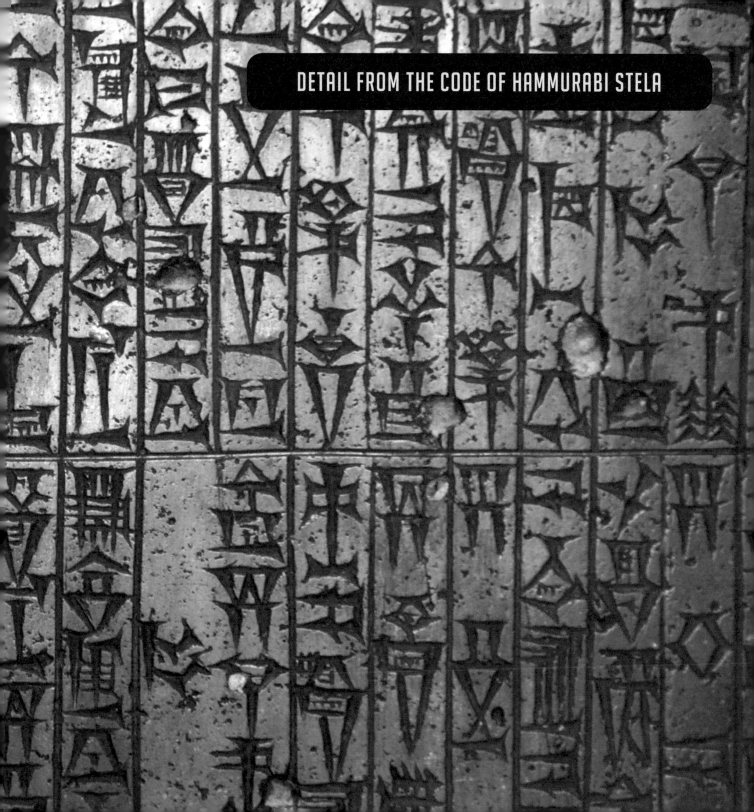
DETAIL FROM THE CODE OF HAMMURABI STELA

CLAY TABLET

Under this king, literature and the arts had new vitality, and the king encouraged preserving and transcribing older clay tablets to not lose their information. He strengthened the army and improved its equipment.

However, not very long later, under one of the sons of Tiglath Pilesar I, Assyria went through an expensive and painful civil war. During this time some territories broke free, and the Aramaeans captured territory in what is now Syria, Israel, and Lebanon. This cut off a major source of wealth that Assyria was relying on. At the same time, the Amorites in Babylon attempted to gain independence.

RUINS OF PALMYRA, SYRIA, BEFORE CIVIL WAR

The Assyrian Empire shrank back over the next century, keeping its home area secure but unable to hold on to the vast territories it had acquired.

THE NEO-ASSYRIAN EMPIRE

Under King Adad Narari II, who ruled from 912 to 891 BCE, Assyria found itself on the path to global conquest again. This is the period when the Assyrians earned the reputation for cruelty and lack of mercy that has stayed with them through history. The Assyrian army was effective and well-equipped, but no more vicious in its time than the Roman legions were a thousand years later.

Among the Assyrians' great advantages were mass-produced iron weapons. They were stronger than the enemies' bronze blades, and could be made more cheaply.

The Assyrians continued their policy of relocating people they conquered, and treating them as members of the empire, not as slaves. Their fierce reputation comes, in part, from the fact that they kept on winning!

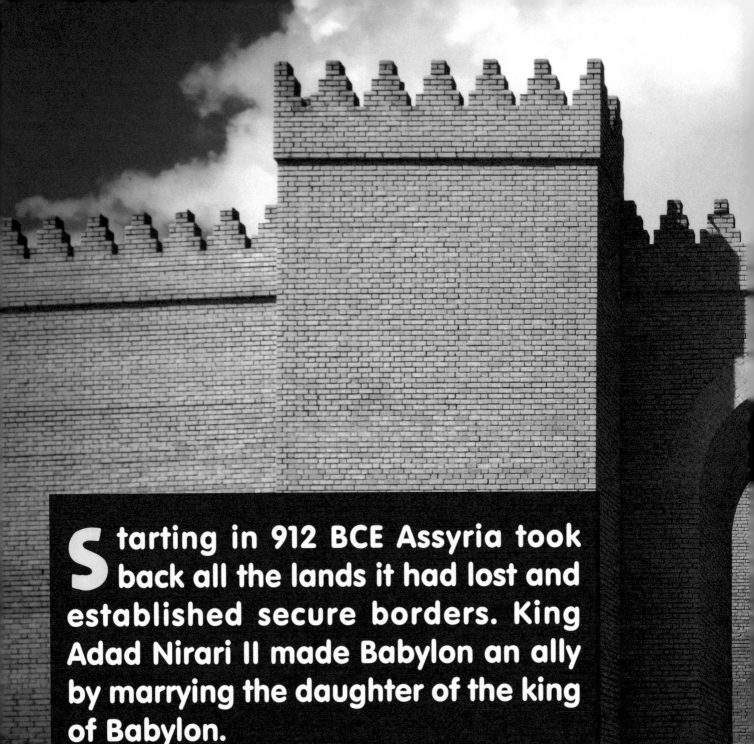

Starting in 912 BCE Assyria took back all the lands it had lost and established secure borders. King Adad Nirari II made Babylon an ally by marrying the daughter of the king of Babylon.

BABYLON GREAT WALLS

MEDITERRANEAN COAST

Assyria concentrated on capturing cities as it expanded this time. It would lay siege to a city and either accept its surrender or destroy its defenses within weeks or months. They had soon expanded their hold on the Mediterranean coast.

Along with military advances, the Assyrians learned more about medicine and healing. There were schools for boys from wealthy and noble families all through the empire. Women could not go to school or hold positions of power.

HARRAN SCHOOL DURING THE ASSYRIAN PERIOD

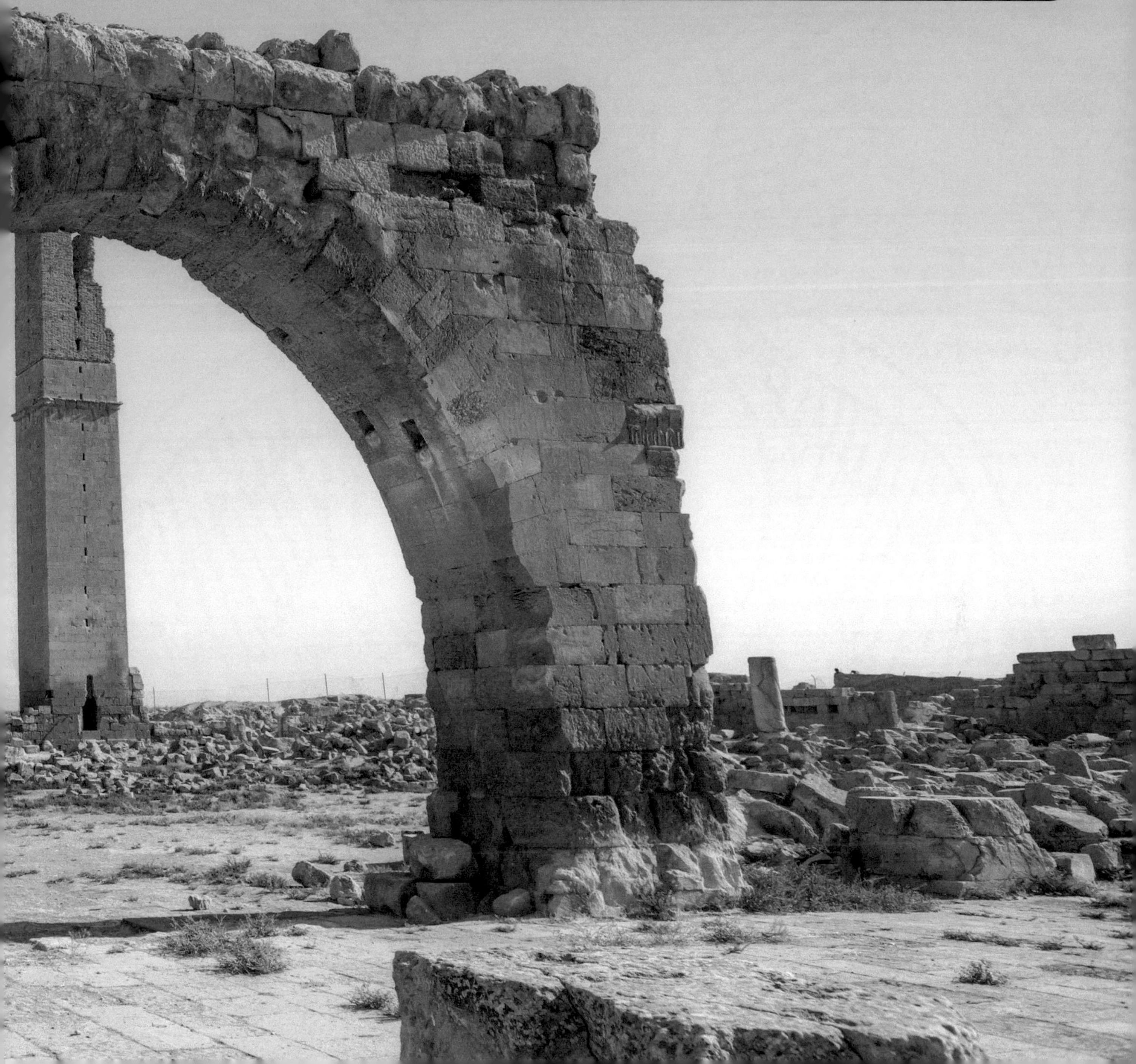

The Assyrians had only worshiped their main god, Ashur, in the temple in their capital city. As the empire expanded, the Assyrians came to understand that the local gods they met in conquered cities might be just local versions of their one god. This is a great move away from a religion that has multiple gods, often quarreling like brothers and sisters in a family. Having a single god, no matter what each part of the empire called him when they worshiped him, helped bring unity to the Assyrians.

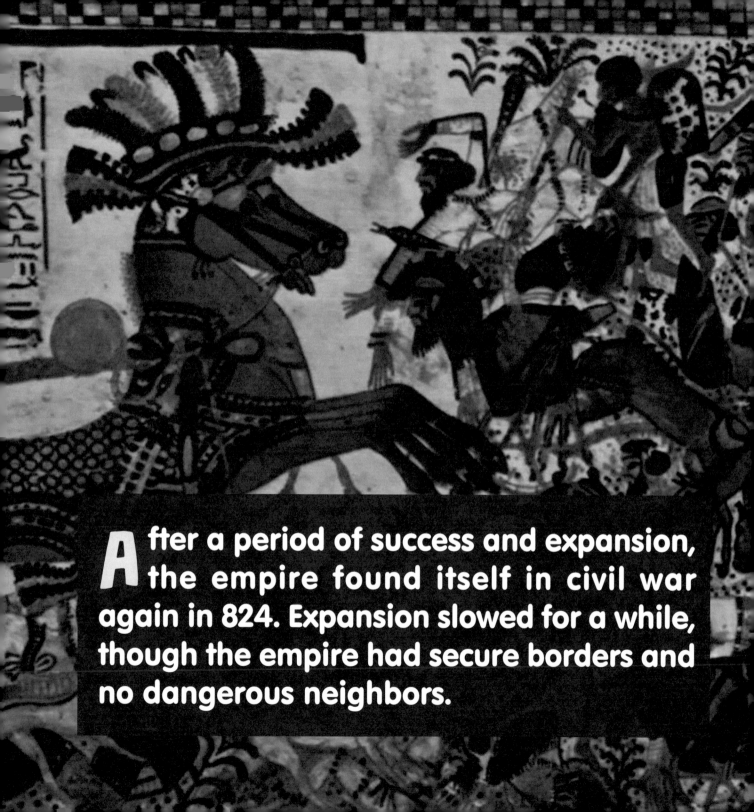

After a period of success and expansion, the empire found itself in civil war again in 824. Expansion slowed for a while, though the empire had secure borders and no dangerous neighbors.

However, when Tiglath Pileser III took the throne in 745 BCE, things heated up again. He improved the structure of the army and of the government, and extended Assyria's control in every direction. His army had become the most efficient and effective force in military history to this point.

Under Sennacherib, who became king in 705, Assyria got a new capital, Ninevah. There the king built what people called "the palace with no equal", and beautiful gardens. Then Sennacherib outraged people by attacking Assyria's ally Babylon and looting its temples. His sons killed him, and the one who took the throne immediately rebuilt Babylon. Soon after, he conquered Egypt and parts of what is now Iran.

THE DEATH OF SENNACHERIB

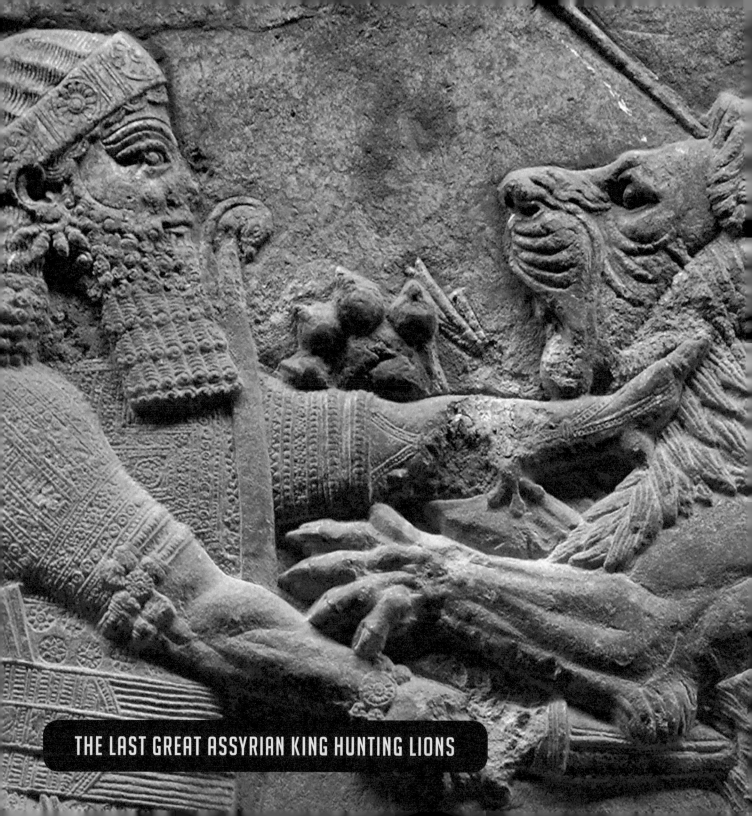

THE LAST GREAT ASSYRIAN KING HUNTING LIONS

The next king, who took the throne in 668 BCE, was Ashurbanipal, Assyria's last great leader. As well as winning military victories, he created a huge library at Ninevah. His reign, which lasted 42 years, was one of success and prosperity.

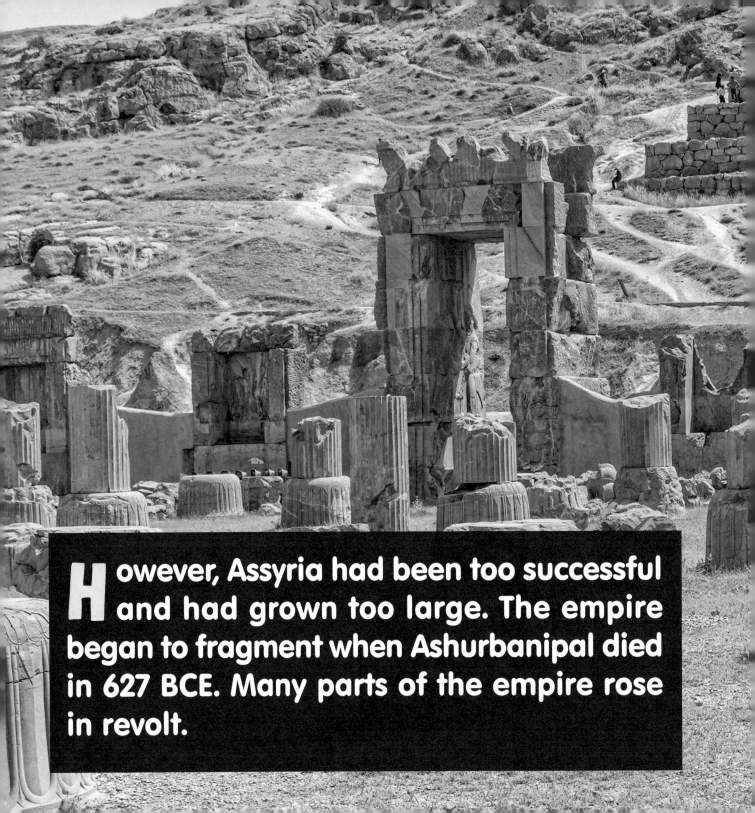

However, Assyria had been too successful and had grown too large. The empire began to fragment when Ashurbanipal died in 627 BCE. Many parts of the empire rose in revolt.

MEDES AND PERSIANS ANCIENT SOLDIERS

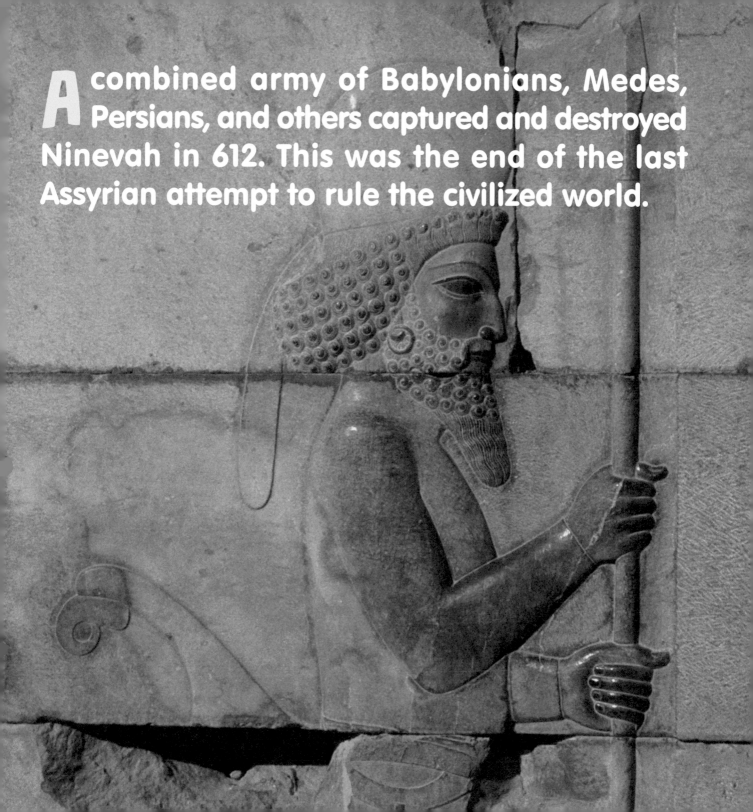

A combined army of Babylonians, Medes, Persians, and others captured and destroyed Ninevah in 612. This was the end of the last Assyrian attempt to rule the civilized world.

THE IMPACT OF ASSYRIA

Within fifty years of the final fall of the Assyrian Empire, people no longer remembered where its great cities like Ninevah and Ashur had been. But the Assyrian people continued, and still live in many nations of the Middle East. Assyrian traditions and innovations helped form every government that followed the Assyrian Empire, right down to today.

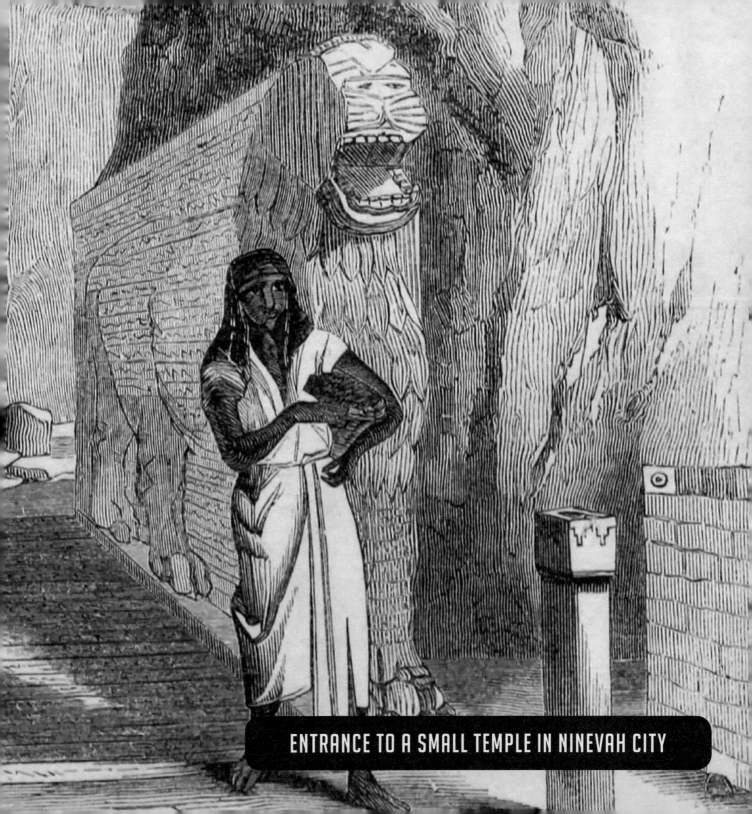

ENTRANCE TO A SMALL TEMPLE IN NINEVAH CITY

Alef
[A]
bull, ox

Beth
[B]
house

Gimel
[G]
stick/camel?

Daleth
[D]
door

Héh
[E]
breath/window?

Waw
[W]
fork, crook, peg

Zaïn
[Z]
arrow, sword

Heth
[H]
wall, fence, field

Theth
[Θ/Th]
wheel

Yodh
[Y]
hand

Kaph
[K]
palm/plant?

Lamed
[L]
goad, whip

Mem
[M]
water

Nun
[N]
snake, eel

Samekh
[S]
fish/support?

Ayïn
[O]
eye

Péh
[P/Ph]
mouth

Tsadi
[C/Ts]
hook/papyrus?

Kof
[Q/Kh]
axe

Resh
[R]
head

Shin
[Š/Sh]
tooth

Taw
[T]
mark

ARAMAIC ALPHABET

Perhaps the Assyrians' biggest contribution was importing the Aramaic alphabet to replace the Akkadian one, and then translating all older documents into this easier writing system. This preserved thousands of years of information about how people lived, what they believed, and how they were governed.

TOUR MESOPOTAMIA!

Learn about the amazing kingdoms and cultures of Mesopotamia in Baby Professor books like Art, Religion and Life in Mesopotamia, Great King Hammurabi and his Code of Law, The Rise and Fall of the Persian Empire, and First Came the Sumerians, Then the Akkadians.

Visit

BABY PROFESSOR
EDUCATION KIDS

www.BabyProfessorBooks.com

to download Free Baby Professor eBooks
and view our catalog of new and exciting
Children's Books

Made in the USA
Thornton, CO
07/05/24 03:47:24

d0023b68-dbaa-4ecb-a759-47cda0a42dacR01